"WE'VE BEEN FRAMED!"

D1562828

"WE'VE BEEN FRAMED!"

Cartoons by Dan Wasserman

Introduction by Pat Oliphant

Faber & Faber / Boston & London / 1987

Printed in the United States of America

Library of Congress Cataloging-in-Publication Data

Wasserman, Dan.
"We've been framed!"

1. United States — Politics and government—1981-Caricatures and cartoons. 2. American wit and humor, Pictorial. I. Title.
E876.W37   1987   973.927'022'2   87-16767
ISBN 0-571-12955-2 (pbk.)

INTRODUCTION

What made a nice young chap like Dan Wasserman leave Washington and move to the People's Republic of Massachusetts and find recognition, fortune, and happiness?

Mind you, around here folks used to call him all kinds of no-good Commie because of his far-left, liberal, bleeding-heart cartoons, and would burn a cross or two on his lawn now and then for good measure. Well, the hell with him if he can't take a joke.

I first met Dan when he visited me in my office at the *Washington Star* during the last days of that paper, and we became friends. I can't imagine why. But he does possess a nicely skewed sense of the ridiculous, as you will see from reading this book. He also laughed at a cartoon I was drawing that day. Nice going, Dan.

Anyway, a couple of years ago, Dan joined the *Boston Globe* as political cartoonist and very quickly hit his proper stride, being reproduced widely in such prestigious journals as the *New York Times,* the *Washington Post,* the *Los Angeles Times,* and the *Philadelphia Inquirer* and also being syndicated by the Los Angeles Times Syndicate. None of this changed him, of course—he stayed the same mean, liberal Commie we all knew in the South. And even in the more civilized climes of the Nor' Nor'-East, his insistence on taking a slash at wrong, both real and perceived, is still getting him into trouble. He takes a stand, expresses it, signs his own name to it, and stands by it. And come hell, high water, and nasty mail, that is what a cartoonist is for.

Dan Wasserman goes from strength to strength and I cheer him all the way, because he understands the uncompromising nature of cartooning well done. I imagine he is young enough, and charged-up enough, to continue in this same vein for many years to come, provided he is not overly concerned about bright lawn ornaments.

But Bostonians wouldn't be so impolite, would they...?

Pat Oliphant
Washington, D.C. 1987

On Oliphant: Pat Oliphant is one of the few rednecks permitted to reside inside the Washington Beltway. He is also a Pulitzer Prize-winning cartoonist who was voted "Best in the Business" by readers of the *Washington Journalism Review* in 1985 and 1987. His drawings are distributed to over 500 newspapers by the Universal Press Syndicate.

A NOTE FROM THE CARTOONIST

I've always been captivated by presidential press conferences. The President walks into a room full of reporters, they all rise, he tells them to sit, they throw questions at him, and he responds with rehearsed answers that may or may not have anything to do with the questions asked. The only thing more one-sided would be if he got to write the questions too. What follows is just such a rigged exchange. I wrote the questions, and I wrote the answers. But, before you cry "foul," let me assure you that the questions were not selected arbitrarily. They are the questions that I am most frequently asked by writers, callers, friends, and budding cartoonists.

Where do you get your ideas?
I get subject matter everywhere—from newspapers, magazines, television, cereal boxes, the neighbors' kids. Anything is grist for the mill. Sometimes ideas spring to life right from a headline, a photo, or an advertising slogan. More often I have to go looking for them. Once you pick a subject, you have to take a clear stand—cartoons can't be built on equivocation. Armed with an opinion, you set off in search of an idea. After a while you learn where they're most likely to hide and you reduce the number of dead ends you go down. The whole process can take from five minutes to five hours, depending on the day.

Are there days when you can't think of anything?
When the news is slow or seems stale, it's hard to come up with something fresh. Your mind is a collection of cliches, your hand doesn't remember how to draw, you suffer from irony-poor blood. The treatment is pacing, caffeine, nicotine, sugar, and more pacing. Something usually comes along. Then there are those terrific days when there's a flood of good material and the problem is choosing among several satisfying ideas.

How did you get started?
With a little luck and a lot of self-addressed stamped envelopes. I was working in Washington, D.C. during the 1980 presidential campaign. I'd been drawing since I was a kid and had always had a fantasy of being a political cartoonist. In its last year of publication, the *Washington Star* opened up a second commentary page and, after much badgering and bundles of unsolicited cartoons, they gave me a space three times a week. The paper folded, but the Los Angeles Times Syndicate had just agreed to distribute my drawings to newspapers around the country. I worked on my own for the next five years before moving to the *Boston Globe.* Having a home paper has made a big difference. Readers

get to see my work consistently over a period of time, and I have a sense of a regular audience.

Who are your favorite politicians to draw?
I have a lot of favorites—Al Haig, Ed Meese, Walter Mondale, George Bush. But Ronald Reagan stands head and shoulders above the rest. That's only in part because he wears plaid suits, reads from cue cards, and sculpts his pompadour with a pint of goop. More importantly, Ronald Reagan brought ideology and political philosophy from the fringes of post-war politics to center stage, and that has fascinated me. He billed himself as a crusader, leader of revolution, pragmatic politics be damned. He hasn't always stuck to that, but he has made explicit his assumptions about government, wealth, and power. He dominated political discussion with a philosophy of unbridled American capitalism, at home and abroad. I disagree with the philosophy, but I think it's good for the country that the debate take place. My cartooning career really began by joining the debate during the 1980 campaign. Reaganism has since revealed itself to be an incompetent and often criminal guide to government, but his opponents have yet to impress the country with an alternative vision and many Democrats are still talking in categories Reagan defined. It almost feels as though he were a character in an ongoing cartoon strip that I draw, and in that sense I'll be sorry to see him leave office.

What cartoons get the most reaction?
Number one is probably cartoons dealing with religious issues. There is a very vocal minority of people that think that no cartoon should ever deal with religion. Often, their angry reactions have little to do with the point of view of the cartoon. They see a Star of David or a cross in a drawing on the editorial page and they reach for the phone or the stationery. In general, local cartoons generate more response than drawings on national or international subjects. People seem to feel closer to local politicians and more strongly about issues in their neighborhoods.

Do your editors tell you what to draw?
No. My cartoons are not an illustration of editorial policy. I develop my own material and at times disagree with the editorials running on the same page. Occasionally, my editors and I wrestle over questions of taste, but those disagreements are rare. Independence is central to serious political cartooning, and I feel fortunate to be able to work with a minimum of interference.

Can cartoons change people's minds?
They sometimes change mine. The struggle to come up with a clear point of view sometimes has surprising results. It's not that you change principles from day to day, but basic principles often conflict. That's the challenge. Are the thoughts in my cartoons affecting readers' thoughts? Cartoonists would like to think so, but it's hard to know. I think they can make people mentally break stride for a moment, long enough to entertain a different way of looking at an issue. That by itself is not going to change someone's way of thinking, but it opens them up to the possibility of change. Cartoons can also declare things publicly that people were thinking only to themselves—people laugh when they see their own thoughts and misgivings captured in a drawing. There is also a morale-boosting role that cartoons can play. For instance, with Reagan's election in 1980, people without money and power were declared unfashionable; a

cartoon can let people know they're not invisible and they're not the only ones who disagree, who are outraged.

What advice do you have for young cartoonists trying to get started?
Draw all the time, but do other things too. Read, travel, get involved politically. Try to find a paper, at school, in the community, that will publish your cartoons. Drawing for publication makes a big difference in how you think about your work. You have to think about communication with an audience and making your ideas clear. Worry more about what you think than about developing a style. Style will develop from your attitude toward issues and from practice. Don't be afraid to experiment. There is no "right" way to draw cartoons.

How do you describe yourself politically?
I used to wrestle with this question. But recently I hit upon the answer—it's all in my book.

A few acknowledgements: Thanks to my parents, Harry and Elga, for teaching me the bad manners necessary to be a cartoonist, to my wife Ellen Edwards for lovingly living with the consequences, to Bob Berger and Eric Seidman of the late *Washington Star* for giving me my start, to my editor Marty Nolan for bringing me to the *Boston Globe* and keeping me there, to Paul Szep for his comradeship, to Pat Oliphant for his ongoing support, to friends and colleagues whom I have drafted to serve as cartoon consultants, and to the readers who take the time to send me brickbats and bouquets.

WAR, LTD.

DESPERATE JOURNEYS

GEORGE — JESSE JACKSON IS MAKING THE U.S. LOOK FOOLISH...

AND CONFUSING THE WORLD ABOUT OUR FOREIGN POLICY

DOES HE HAVE THE RIGHT TO DO THAT?

NO, SIR — THAT'S _YOUR_ JOB

WASSERMAN © 1984 LOS ANGELES TIMES SYNDICATE

WHAT IS THE DIFFERENCE BETWEEN TOTALITARIAN AND AUTHORITARIAN?

WELL, A TOTALITARIAN GOVERNMENT ARRESTS, TORTURES AND MURDERS

AN AUTHORITARIAN GOVERNMENT, ON THE OTHER HAND...

LEAVES MANY OF THESE FUNCTIONS TO THE PRIVATE SECTOR

WASSERMAN ©'81

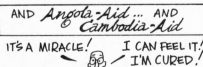

THE RECENT DISTURBANCES BROKE OUT IN SMALL TOWNS AND LARGE CITIES

THEY INVOLVED WORKERS AND STUDENTS, MEN AND WOMEN, YOUNG AND OLD

AND EVERYWHERE THE SLOGANS AND DEMANDS WERE EXACTLY THE SAME

FELLOW POLES — THIS IS CLEARLY A CONSPIRACY!

WASSERMAN
© 1982 L.A. TIMES SYNDICATE

I THOUGHT WE KILLED ALL THE COMMUNISTS

DEMOCRACY NOW
DEMOCRACY
FREE ELECTIONS
DEMOCRACY
DEMOCRACY
ELECTIONS NOW
CHILEANS WANT DEMOCRACY!

WASSERMAN
© 1984 L.A. TIMES SYNDICATE

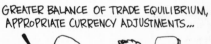

ANGOLA IN THE NEWS →

RONALD REAGAN WANTS TO GIVE AID...

TO A CHINESE-TRAINED GUERRILLA...

WHO IS BANKROLLED BY SOUTH AFRICA...

TO MAKE ATTACKS ON U.S.-OWNED OIL REFINERIES...

WHICH ARE GUARDED BY CUBAN TROOPS...

AT THE REQUEST OF THE MARXIST ANGOLAN GOVERNMENT.

THE WHITE HOUSE WANTS THE SUPPORT OF THE U.S. PEOPLE.

WASSERMAN © '86 THE BOSTON GLOBE L.A. TIMES SYND.

WE WANT YOU BLACK SOUTH AFRICANS TO KNOW WE'RE WITH YOU...

BUT DON'T BE TOO IMPATIENT WITH YOUR GOVERNMENT

PRESIDENT BOTHA SAYS HE TRULY WANTS TO END APARTHEID...

AND FOR THAT WE APPLAUD HIM

CLAP CLAP

WASSERMAN THE BOSTON GLOBE © '86 L.A. TIMES SYND.

I'M IN CHARGE OF OUR CONSTRUCTIVE ENGAGEMENT POLICY TOWARD SOUTH AFRICA

MY JOB IS TO POINT TO PROGRESS... HAIL REFORMS AND URGE RESTRAINT

I CLAIM SUCCESSES... OBJECT TO SANCTIONS... EMPHASIZE THE POSITIVE...

AND DEPLORE MASSACRES AS OFTEN AS NECESSARY

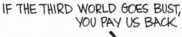

AS THE POLLS TURN

I CAN'T BELIEVE IT—
A HOLLYWOOD ACTOR
COMES INTO
WASHINGTON
FOR THE FIRST
TIME

AND PROCEEDS TO
COMMUNICATE LIKE
FDR, TO CHARM
LIKE JFK...

AND TO PLAY POLITICAL
HARDBALL LIKE
LYNDON JOHNSON

HE MUST BE USING
STUNT MEN

THANKS ED... WE
OPEN OUR 1982
SEASON WITH
ANOTHER GREAT
SHOW—

DAVE STOCKMAN WILL
TELL US ABOUT HIS
NEW SELF-HELP
BOOK FOR THE POOR—
"DRESS FOR
SUCCESS"

PAUL VOLCKER HAS
SOME TIPS FOR YOU
HOME-BUYERS ON
LIVING IN
YOUR
CAR

AND I'LL BE
READING YOU SOME
OF OUR FAN MAIL
FROM NURSING HOMES
AROUND THE
COUNTRY

WE'LL BE RIGHT BACK
AFTER THIS IMPORTANT
WORD FROM THE FOLKS
AT THE PENTAGON

DON'T MISS THE NEXT EPISODE OF –

AS THE POLLS TURN

IS AMERICA SERIOUSLY INVOLVED WITH A **YOUNGER MAN**?

OR WILL SHE FIND HAPPINESS WITH HER **FORMER NUMBER TWO**?

WHO IS THE **LEGITIMATE** SON OF FDR?

WHAT DID THIS MAN FIND OUT AND **WHEN**?

EXIT POLLS

TUNE IN EVERY TUESDAY, EVERY WEEK, PRACTICALLY **FOREVER**

WASSERMAN ©1984 LOS ANGELES TIMES SYNDICATE

TELL ME SOMETHING — WOULD JESSE JACKSON EVEN BE A PRESIDENTIAL CANDIDATE...

IF IT WEREN'T FOR THE FACT THAT HE'S <u>BLACK</u>?

WELL... TELL ME SOMETHING—

WOULD RONALD REAGAN BE PRESIDENT IF HE WEREN'T WHITE?

WASSERMAN ©1984 LOS ANGELES TIMES SYNDICATE

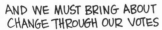

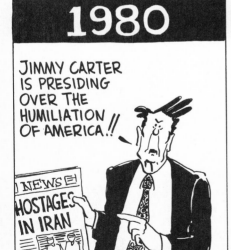

SAY "UNCLE"

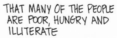

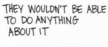

THIS IS OUR MISSION— WE WILL RUN AN OPERATION AGAINST NICARAGUA THAT VIOLATES U.S. LAW

WE WILL KEEP THE AMERICAN PUBLIC IN THE DARK ABOUT OUR ACTIVITIES

WE WILL BRING TO THE NICARAGUAN PEOPLE THE NATIONAL GUARD THEY JUST THREW OUT

DO WE HAVE A CODE NAME?

PROJECT DEMOCRACY

WASSERMAN © 1983 LOS ANGELES TIMES SYNDICATE

MR. LEFEVER, HOW WOULD YOU DEAL WITH TORTURE AND MURDER BY RIGHT-WING DICTATORSHIPS?

QUIET DIPLOMACY, SENATOR

COULD YOU GIVE US AN EXAMPLE?

I'M SORRY, I DIDN'T CATCH THAT

IT'S MILITARY LINGO, SENATOR

WASSERMAN © '81

MILLIONS ARE MARCHING AGAINST OUR MISSILES IN EUROPE

WE'VE GOT OUR MARINES TRAPPED IN LEBANON

AND WE'RE GETTING NOWHERE IN CENTRAL AMERICA

INVADE GRENADA!!

WASSERMAN ©1983 LOS ANGELES TIMES SYNDICATE

WE HAVE CAPTURED SECRET CUBAN MILITARY DOCUMENTS IN GRENADA

THEY CONTAIN PLANS FOR A CUBAN MILITARY BUILDUP ON THE ISLAND...

AND THEY REVEAL THE JUSTIFICATION THAT WAS GOING TO BE USED FOR THE BUILDUP—

THE THREAT OF A U.S. INVASION

WASSERMAN © 1983 LOS ANGELES TIMES SYNDICATE

THE NICARAGUANS ARE CONSORTING WITH LIBYA, IRAN AND THE PLO!!

ALL OUR FRIENDS IN THE REGION ARE CLEAN-CUT ALL-AMERICAN TYPES

THE LAW DEALS WITH SMUGGLERS OF ILLEGAL ALIENS:

WINK!

GROWERS

CLINK!

SANCTUARY MOVEMENT

COMRADE — CAN YOU THINK OF A WAY TO BRING NICARAGUA CLOSER TO US...

UNDERMINE THEIR CAPITALIST PRIVATE SECTOR...

AND PROVIDE EXCUSES FOR THEIR ECONOMIC FAILURES?

DA — A U.S. TRADE EMBARGO

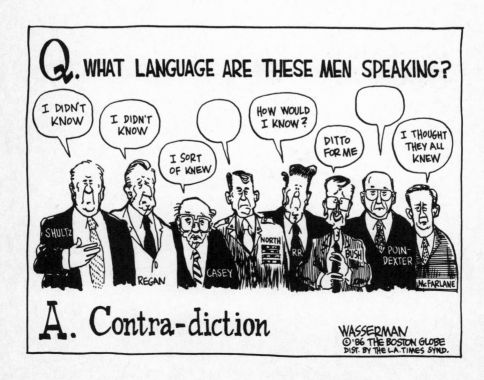

LET THEM EAT JUNK BONDS

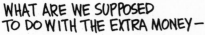

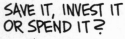

THE PRESIDENT CUT MY SCHOOL LUNCH

BUT HE DID IT FOR MY OWN GOOD

HE WANTS ME TO KNOW THAT BEING POOR IS NO FUN

THAT YOU CAN'T GET SOMETHING FOR NOTHING

AND THAT YOU HAVE TO WORK VERY HARD...

BEFORE YOU CAN DEDUCT LUNCH FROM YOUR TAXES

WASSERMAN © '81

WELCOME TO OUR LIVE COVERAGE OF THE ECONOMIC RECOVERY OF 1982

THE ADMINISTRATION EXPECTS THIS LINE TO HEAD UPWARD ANY MOMENT

THERE IT GOES! THIS IS IT! THE ECONOMIC RECOVERY!

BLIP!

WASSERMAN

© 1982 L.A. TIMES SYNDICATE

WE'LL BE RIGHT BACK WITH THE INSTANT REPLAY

TO SIMPLIFY THE FIGHT OVER THE BUDGET CUTS,

WE'RE PLANNING AN ELIMINATION TOURNAMENT...

THE FARMERS CAN TAKE ON THE ELDERLY, THE JOBLESS VS. THE SCHOOLKIDS, ETC.

THE WINNER GETS TO GO ONE-ON-ONE WITH THE PENTAGON

WASSERMAN © '81

MR. MAYOR — THIS IS HOW OUR FISCAL MAGIC WORKS

YOUR FEDERAL AID BUNNY GOES IN THIS HAT

I SAY THE MAGIC WORDS — BLOCK GRANT-SLASH! AND THE SPELL IS CAST

GOOD LUCK!

WASSERMAN © '81

THIS IS A TIME OF DIFFICULT CHANGES IN OUR ECONOMY...

AND THESE CHANGES CALL FOR A NEW RELATIONSHIP BETWEEN MANAGEMENT AND LABOR

I AM THEREFORE PREPARED TO MAKE YOU THE FOLLOWING PROPOSITION—

YOUR MONEY OR YOUR JOB

WASSERMAN © 1982 LOS ANGELES TIMES SYNDICATE

LET ME SAY A FEW SPECIAL WORDS TO THOSE OF YOU WHO ARE UNEMPLOYED

WHEN YOU START TO FEEL DISHEARTENED, THERE'S SOMETHING YOU SHOULD REMEMBER—

EACH OF YOU, INDIVIDUALLY, MAY BE JUST ANOTHER PERSON WITHOUT A JOB...

BUT TAKEN TOGETHER, YOU'RE 10.3 MILLION INFLATION FIGHTERS!

WASSERMAN © 1982 L.A. TIMES SYNDICATE

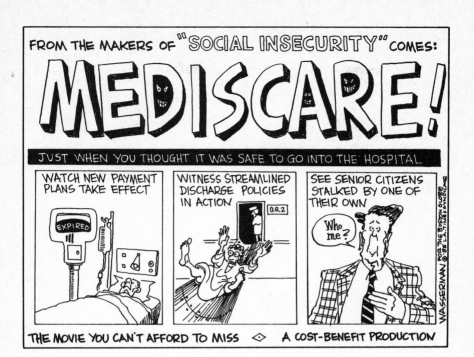

HYSTERICAL ENVIRONMENTALISTS WANT NEW SAFETY CHECKS ON U.S. PLANTS

NUCLEAR INDUSTRY

WHY? — BECAUSE OF THE ACCIDENT AT CHERNOBYL

BUT THAT ACCIDENT HAS NOTHING TO DO WITH OUR PLANTS

WHY? — BECAUSE OUR REACTORS HAVE CONTAINERS

WHY? — BECAUSE OF...

HYSTERICAL ENVIRONMENTALISTS

WASSERMAN THE BOSTON GLOBE ©'86 L.A. TIMES SYND.

MR. MILLER, YOU CALL FOR CUTS IN FOOD STAMPS, MEDICAID, NUTRITION AND JOB TRAINING

OMB

HOW DOES THAT SQUARE WITH THE PRESIDENT'S PLEDGE NOT TO BALANCE THE BUDGET...

ON THE BACK OF THE MAN WHO IS POOR?

CONGRESSMAN — THESE CUTS WOULD AFFECT MOSTLY WOMEN AND CHILDREN

WASSERMAN FOR THE BOSTON GLOBE ©'86 L.A. TIMES SYND.

SEX, DRUGS, AND ED MEESE

WE HAVE DEALT A DEVASTATING BLOW TO THE FORCES OF EVIL —

THE LIBERTINE LIBERALS HAVE BEEN SWEPT FROM OFFICE

AND NOW THAT WE'VE STRAIGHTENED OUT MOST OF THE LEGISLATURES...

WE CAN GET STARTED ON THE LIBRARIES

IT'S TIME TO TAKE THE CUFFS OFF THE CIA...

AND AUTHORIZE DOMESTIC SURVEILLANCE AND INFILTRATION

THERE ARE PEOPLE WHO CHARGE IT COULD BECOME A SECRET POLICE

LAST NAMES FIRST

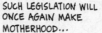

OUTLAWING ABORTION IS NOT ANTI-WOMAN – IT'S PRO-FAMILY

SUCH LEGISLATION WILL ONCE AGAIN MAKE MOTHERHOOD...

RESPECTED, CHERISHED, HONORED...

AND MANDATORY

WASSERMAN © '81

HELLO- I'D LIKE TO GIVE YOU OUR PERSPECTIVE ON RECENT CIGARETTE REGULATIONS

TOBACCO INDUSTRY

A NEW LAW REQUIRES US TO ROTATE HEALTH WARNINGS ON ADS AND WRAPPERS

TOBACCO INDUSTRY

EACH LABEL WILL DESCRIBE A DIFFERENT HAZARD OF SMOKING

TOBACCO INDUSTRY

OUR POSITION IS – START NOW AND COLLECT THEM ALL !!

TOBAC INDU

WASSERMAN FOR THE BOSTON GLOBE © '86 L.A. TIMES SYND.

AS SOON AS THE ARTIFICIAL HEART IS IN PLACE, START THE PRESS CONFERENCE

GIVE THE MEDIA THE WORKS — MEDICAL STATS, PHOTOS, VIDEOS, HUMAN INTEREST ANGLES

WHAT ABOUT THE PATIENT'S PRIVACY?

OH, WE REMOVE THAT AS PART OF THE OPERATION

THE CBS EVENING NEWS WITH JESSE HELMS

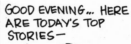

GOOD EVENING... HERE ARE TODAY'S TOP STORIES—

LIBERALS LINKED TO LUNG CANCER... BOLSHOI CAUGHT CHEATING...

RESEARCH SHOWS WOMEN HAPPIER AT HOME...

SALVADORAN RIGHTIST PLEADS INNOCENT TO PARKING TICKET...

AND A SPECIAL REPORT— WHO PAINTED AMERICA'S SCHOOLHOUSES RED?

See Dick
See Jane

See Dick run
See Jane run

See Jane's
belly grow

See Jane drop out
of school

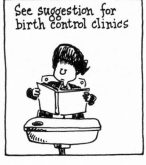

See suggestion for
birth control clinics

See politicians
run

REMEMBER IN THE 60's WE WERE ALWAYS LOOKING FOR THE ISSUE THAT COULD AROUSE THE MASSES?

THE CAUSE THAT WOULD BRING MILLIONS INTO THE STREETS TO MARCH AGAINST CORPORATE TYRANNY

WELL, BROTHER, WE FINALLY HAVE THE ISSUE

SOUTH AFRICA?

NEW COKE

WASSERMAN ©1985 LOS ANGELES TIMES SYNDICATE

DOES THE SUPREME COURT GIVE YOU A PAIN?

MEESE

DOES IT OVERTURN LAWS YOU LIKE AND UPHOLD ONES YOU HATE?

WRITE AWAY NOW FOR MY FREE BOOKLET

DO-IT-YOURSELF CONSTITUTIONAL LAW

THIS HANDY GUIDE LETS YOU MAKE YOUR OWN RULINGS

DON'T LET THOSE NINE KNOW-IT-ALLS TELL YOU WHAT THE LAW IS!

THEY'VE BEEN CHANGING THEIR MINDS FOR 200 YEARS!

WASSERMAN THE BOSTON GLOBE © '86 LA TIMES SYND.

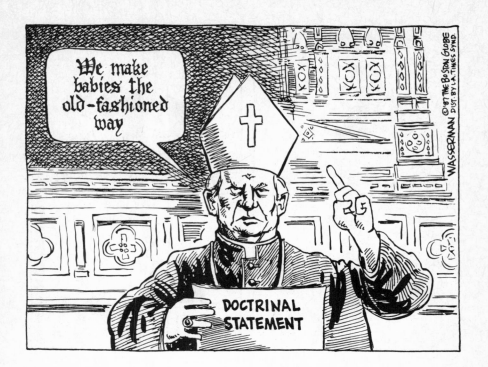

POSSIBLE REAGAN SUPREME COURT NOMINEES

OLIVER NORTH: Conservative, energetic experienced in legal opinions.

TAMMY BAKKER: A woman, understands social issues, needs the money.

BERNHARD GOETZ: Law and order advocate, persuasive in small groups.

ATTY. GEN'L. ED MEESE: (Just kidding.)

MASS.
PRODUCTIONS

"MY INSURANCE COMPANY? NEW ENGLAND LIFE, OF COURSE."

DON'T YOU THINK BOSTON NEEDS A DEVELOPMENT PLAN?

B.R.A.

A PLAN? YES-SO THE CITY ISN'T DESIGNED BY DEVELOPERS AND SPECULATORS

WITHOUT A PLAN, WHAT RULES DO WE HAVE?

THE RULES ACCORDING TO COYLE!!

A PILOT T.V. SPOT FOR CAMPAIGN '88...